to the amazing
Matt Man.

10/17/88 BET $595

74119

92      91      90      89      88              5       4       3       2       1

Library of Congress Catalog Card Number: 88–070250

International Standard Book Number: 0–933893–51–5

**Bonus Books, Inc.**
160 East Illinois Street, Chicago, Illinois 60611


*Printed in the United States of America*

*For Quantity Discounts*

Bonus Books publications are available at quantity discounts with bulk purchase for educational, business or sales promotional use. For information, please write:   Special Sales Department
Bonus Books, Inc.
160 E. Illinois
Chicago, IL 60611

# It's never too early to start worrying

**Shoe** By Jeff MacNelly

YOU'RE HEADED DOWN TO SPRING TRAINING?

OF COURSE.

FANS HAVE TO GET IN SHAPE FOR THE SEASON, TOO.

I STILL DON'T SEE WHY YOU GO DOWN TO SPRING TRAINING.

WELL, IT'S NOT JUST ANOTHER SILLY RITUAL OF SPORTS, SKYLER.

SPRING TRAINING IS BASIC HUMAN DRAMA.

THERE YOU ARE, THE AGING VETERAN, WONDERING IF YOU STILL HAVE IT.

YOU WONDER IF YOU CAN GET YOUR BODY IN SHAPE FOR YET ANOTHER SUMMER CAMPAIGN.

SO YOU GO TO SPRING TRAINING TO TUNE YOUR BODY, TO HONE YOUR SKILLS, REBUILD YOUR STAMINA...

© Jefferson Communications, Inc. 1986
Distributed by Tribune Media Services, Inc.

TO FIND OUT IF YOU STILL HAVE ENOUGH OF THE OLD MOVES...

TO SEE IF YOU STILL HAVE ONE MORE SEASON LEFT IN YOU...

YUP. LOOKS LIKE I MADE THE CUT AGAIN THIS YEAR...

By Jeff MacNelly

HEY, IRVING... I GOT AN EXTRA TICKET TO TODAY'S CUBS GAME. —WANNA COME?

SURE!

LET ME CHECK WITH THE WIFE.

HONEY? IS IT OKAY IF I GO TO THE CUBS GAME WITH PERFESSER?

¿ SIGH ?

SHE SAYS I CAN GO.

AH, MARRIAGE!

OKAY, SO THESE AREN'T THE BEST SEATS TO WATCH THE BALL GAME...

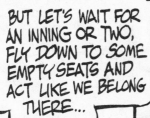

BUT LET'S WAIT FOR AN INNING OR TWO, FLY DOWN TO SOME EMPTY SEATS AND ACT LIKE WE BELONG THERE...

HEY, THERE'S TWO, AND THEY'RE RIGHT IN FRONT.

DON'T JUST SIT THERE, GRAB SOME BEECHNUT AND START SPITTIN'...

© Jefferson Communications, Inc. 1985
Distributed by Tribune Media Services, Inc.

SEE? THESE AREN'T SUCH BAD SEATS...

ARE YOU KIDDING?

HE MISSED THE TAG!! HE MISSED THE TAG!!

EVEN BOB UECKER IS IN FRONT OF US...

© Jefferson Communications, Inc. 1985
Distributed by Tribune Media Services, Inc.

# SHOE

### BY Jeff MacNelly

WHAT A BEAUTIFUL DAY...

...TO SNEAK OFF TO THE BALL GAME.

I'M WORKIN' A STORY.... I'LL BE GONE THE REST OF THE AFTERNOON.

RIGHT.

NOW'S MY CHANCE TO SLIP OFF TO THE BALLPARK.

KNOW WHAT YOU GET WHEN YOU MIX A BEAUTIFUL DAY WITH AN ABSENT BOSS...

AND A PAIR OF SEATS TO THE AFTERNOON GAME?...

I GNE UP.

"THE LUNCH OF NO RETURN."

MacNelly 5/7

YOU WORRY TOO MUCH, UNCLE COSMO...

IT'S ONLY THE FOURTH INNING OF THE OPENING GAME.

I'M REASONABLY SURE WE CAN'T GO HITLESS FOR THE ENTIRE SEASON.

MacNelly 4/8

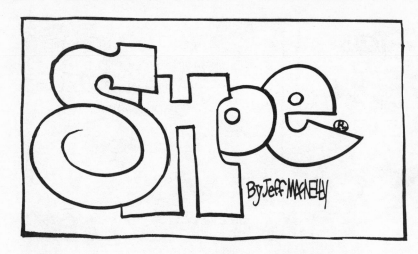

As their relief pitcher saunters to the mound...

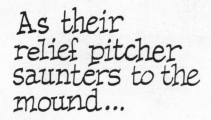

...the ground crew begins to cover the infield with tarp...

...proof the Cubs take Lefty's notorious spitball very seriously.

PRESS BOX

MACNELLY

Sports Dept.

By Jeff MacNelly

HEAD SPORT

Boston Destroys New York, 14-2.

Milwaukee Bashes A's, 10-1; 12-0.

Baltimore Decapitates White Sox, 11-1.

Padres Rip Guts Out of L.A., 15-0.

Mets Murder Giants, 17-2.

Jefferson Communications, Inc. 1984
Distributed by Tribune Media Services, Inc

Cubs Demolish St. Louis, 14-2.

Rangers Eaten Alive By Indians, 13-0.

?

Pirates Quite Rude to Atlanta, 4-1.

7/29

WHAT THE HECK, IT'S JUST A GAME.

## Other Bonus Books baseball titles:

### COLLECTING BASEBALL CARDS

by Donn Pearlman

This new edition of a bestseller includes a *free* baseball card in each book. Beginners as well as advanced card collectors and investors will learn the best way to buy, sell, and trade cards.
**Paperback, $6.95**

### THE GOLDEN ERA CUBS: 1876-1940
### THE NEW ERA CUBS: 1941-1985

by Eddie Gold and Art Ahrens

"What fun it is to have those Cub heroes parade past us once again. What a pleasure to supplement the memories and anecdotes we know about them with even more interesting stories we've never known before. . . You don't have to go far to get hooked on this book." – Jack Brickhouse
**THE GOLDEN ERA CUBS**
**– hardcover, $12.95**
**THE NEW ERA CUBS**
**– hardcover, $14.95**

### BLEEP! LARRY BOWA MANAGES

by Larry Bowa with Barry Bloom

In BLEEP!, former Cubs star Larry Bowa tells the dramatic story of his struggles and frustrations as first-year manager of the San Diego Padres. He is known for being outspoken and controversial and lives up to that reputation in this revealing book.
**Hardcover, $15.95**

**At your local bookstore –**

**or**
**use the handy coupon on the next page for ordering.**

# ORDER FORM

☐ THE NEW ERA CUBS, $14.95
☐ THE GOLDEN ERA CUBS, $12.95
☐ COLLECTING BASEBALL CARDS, $6.95
☐ BLEEP! LARRY BOWA MANAGES, $15.95

Add $3 for shipping and handling

Name _____
Address _____
City _____ State _____ Zip _____
Telephone _____
☐ Visa   ☐ Mastercard   ☐ American Express   ☐ Check enclosed
Account # _____ Expiration date _____
Signature _____
Shipping instructions: All books sent U.P.S. unless otherwise indicated.
Allow 1-2 weeks for delivery.

Mail this order form to: **Bonus Books**
160 E. Illinois St.
Chicago, IL 60611

### Or order toll free:
1-800-225-3775
312-467-0580 (in Illinois)